**SCHOLASTIC**

# Scholastic Success With
# Spelling

## by Lisa Molengraft

New York • Toronto • London • Auckland • Sydney
Mexico City • New Delhi • Hong Kong • Buenos Aires

**Teaching** *Resources*

Cover art by Amy Vangsgard
Cover design by Maria Lilja
Interior illustrations by Sherry Neidigh
Interior design by Quack & Company

ISBN 0-7172-9921-X

12 11 10 9 8 7 6 5 4 3 2 1        06 07 08 09 10/0

Scholastic Teaching Resources

# Introduction

Parents and teachers alike will find this book to be a valuable learning tool. The book is organized into 21 lists, each following a phonetic spelling rule. The list words were developed from a collection of age-appropriate, high-priority word lists. At the end of each list you will find three words that can be used as an academic challenge.

Throughout the book you will find the following symbols that represent various strategy-based skills:

 **Visual Discrimination Skills:** *Use this strategy to highlight visual similarities among words.*

 **Sound Relationship Skills:** *Use this strategy to highlight sound patterns among words.*

 **Dictation Skills:** *Read the dictation sentence aloud to students. Having students write the sentence will provide additional practice in spelling list words as well as practice in using correct punctuation.*

 **Writing Skills:** *Use this strategy to practice writing sentences using the list words.*

 **Reading Skills:** *These activities include stories and letters with missing words, giving students an opportunity to connect reading with writing.*

 **Fun Stuff!:** *This section includes games, puzzles, and codes in which children apply previously learned strategies.*

 **Challenge Word Activities:** *This section offers an opportunity to stretch spelling skills to a more difficult level using the three optional challenge words.*

 **Bright Idea Activities:** *This section offers extension ideas to bridge beyond "the book" and into "the world."*

Throughout the book students will find Review Lists. These are not a collection of "old words," but are actually new list words that follow previously learned patterns. This list gives students a chance to apply mastered skills and strategies.

Through a collection of well-prepared lists, age-appropriate challenges, valuable spelling strategies, and stimulating activities, students will gain the self-confidence they need to become strong spellers.

# Table of Contents

**Matt's Map** *(Short-*a *sound)* . . . . . . . . . . . . . . . . . .4

**My Backyard Tent** *(Short-*e *sound)* . . . . . . . . . . .6

**The Missed Kick** *(Short-*i *sound)* . . . . . . . . . . . . . .8

**Socks With Dots** *(Short-*o *sound)* . . . . . . . . . . . .10

**A Bump in the Road** *(Short-*u *sound)* . . . . . . . .12

**Who Dropped the Ball?** *(Short vowel sounds/* -ing *and* -ed *endings)* . . . . . . . . . . . . . . . . . . . . .14

**A Snake on the Trail** *(Long-*a *sound)* . . . . . . . .16

**A Sleepy Team** *(Long-*e *sound)* . . . . . . . . . . . . . .18

**The Night Sky** *(Long-*i *sound)* . . . . . . . . . . . . . . .20

**Let It Snow!** *(Long-*o *sound)* . . . . . . . . . . . . . . . . .22

**Deep in the Hole** *(Review)* . . . . . . . . . . . . . . . . . .24

**The Cute Mule** *(Long-*u *sound)* . . . . . . . . . . . . . .26

**A True Blue Friend** *(Long-*u *sound)* . . . . . . . . . .28

**A Good Book** *(Short* oo *sound)* . . . . . . . . . . . . . .30

**Which White Shell?** *(Digraphs* sh, ch, th, *and* wh) . . . . . . . . . . . . . . . . . . . . . . . . . . . . . . .32

**A Clue to the Treasure Chest** *(Review)* . . . . . . .34

**The Hurt Bird** *(*r-Controlled vowels*)* . . . . . . . . .36

**The Clown's House** *(Diphthongs* ow *and* ou*)* . .38

**Enjoy the Toy!** *(Diphthongs* oi *and* oy*)* . . . . . . .40

**There Goes the Ball!** *(Differentiating* aw *and* all*)* . . . . . . . . . . . . . . . . . . . . . . . . . . . . . . . . .42

**The Girl's Small Horse** *(Review)* . . . . . . . . . . . . .44

**Master Spelling List** . . . . . . . . . . . . . . . . . . . . . . .46

**Answer Key** . . . . . . . . . . . . . . . . . . . . . . . . . . . . . .47

Scholastic Teaching Resources

# Matt's Map

The **short-**a **sound** *is found in the word* **map**.

Read and copy each list word. Circle the letter that makes the short-*a* sound. Watch for a word with an unexpected silent *e* ending. Then organize the list words by their number of letters.

 **List Words**

| | | three letters | five letters |
|---|---|---|---|
| 1. map | 1. _____ | _____ | _____ |
| 2. ask | 2. _____ | _____ | _____ |
| 3. last | 3. _____ | _____ | |
| 4. has | 4. _____ | **four letters** | |
| 5. sack | 5. _____ | | |
| 6. clap | 6. _____ | _____ | |
| 7. after | 7. _____ | _____ | |
| 8. mask | 8. _____ | _____ | |
| 9. black | 9. _____ | _____ | |
| 10. have | 10. _____ | _____ | |

**Challenge Words**

11. backpack    11. _____

12. stamp    12. _____

13. stand    13. _____

Change one letter in each word to spell a list word. The first one has been done for you.

1. ash _*ask*_

2. mash _____

3. slap _____

4. block _____

5. list _____

6. lap _____

7. his _____

8. sick _____

9. hive _____

Matt has a map in the black sack.

Use the list words to complete the story.

**Matt's Map**

Matt _____ a map of the houses on his

street. He keeps the map in his _____ sack. _____ night Matt could

not find his map. He looked everywhere. "Do you _____ my map?" he

would _____ everyone. Matt saw something under his Halloween

_____. It was his _____! Matt was so happy he began to _____.

_____ that, Matt always put his map back in his black _____.

:) Follow the clues to play tic-tac-toe. As you find each answer, mark an
*X* or *O*. Do you get three in a row?

**1.** I am the antonym (opposite) for *answer*. Mark an *X*.

**2.** I am a color. Mark an *O*.

**3.** I rhyme with *past*. Mark an *X*.

**4.** I am the antonym for *before*. Mark an *O*.

**5.** She _____ a sister. Mark an *X*.

**6.** I begin like the word *sit*. Mark an *X*.

**7.** I rhyme with *map*. Mark an *X*.

**8.** They _____ a dog. Mark an *O*.

**9.** I rhyme with *ask*. Mark an *X*.

| has | have | clap |
|------|------|------|
| black | mask | sack |
| last | after | ask |

⭐ Write the challenge word that finishes each analogy.

**10.** You put a plate on the table. You put a _____ on a letter.

**11.** *Down* is the antonym for *up*. *Sit* is the antonym for _____.

**12.** A wallet is kept in a purse. A book is kept in a _____.

 **Cut letters from an old newspaper and glue them to another sheet of paper to spell each of the list words.**

Name _____

# My Backyard Tent

 *The* **short-*e*** **sound** *is found in the word* **tent**.

Read and copy each list word. Circle the letter that makes the short-*e* sound. Watch for a word with an unexpected spelling. Then organize the list words by their ending letters.

### List Words

|  |  | | words that end with *t* | words that end with *d* |
|---|---|---|---|---|
| 1. tent | 1. _____ | | | |
| 2. met | 2. _____ | | _____ | _____ |
| 3. send | 3. _____ | | _____ | _____ |
| 4. went | 4. _____ | | _____ | _____ |
| 5. bed | 5. _____ | | _____ | _____ |
| 6. nest | 6. _____ | | _____ | _____ |
| 7. bend | 7. _____ | | _____ | |
| 8. yet | 8. _____ | | _____ | |
| 9. best | 9. _____ | | | |
| 10. said | 10. _____ | | | |

### Challenge Words

| 11. bench | 11. _____ |
|---|---|
| 12. next | 12. _____ |
| 13. else | 13. _____ |

Each list word has a rhyming partner. Write two list words that rhyme.

1. _____      2. _____      3. _____

_____      _____      _____

4. _____      5. _____

_____      _____

 "I **went** to **bed** in a **tent**," said **Ned**.

Circle ten misspelled words. Write them correctly on the lines.

## My Backyard Tent

My dad and I built a tint in the backyard. We had to bind sticks to stake it in the ground. We had the beste time. We made a bid out of straw. We sed it was like a bird's nast. My mom said she would sind a snack out to us. We mete her in the yard and then she whent back in the house. She said she isn't ready for camping yat!

1. _____  2. _____  3. _____  4. _____

5. _____  6. _____  7. _____  8. _____

9. _____  10. _____

Use addition and subtraction to spell each list word. The first one has been done for you.

11. rest – r + b = ___*best*___     12. test – s + n = _____

13. mat – a + e = _____     14. bad – a + e = _____

15. sent – t + d = _____    16. sand – n + i = _____

17. send – s + b = _____    18. set – s + y = _____

19. next – x + s = _____    20. want – a + e = _____

Write the challenge word that matches each definition.

21. another choice _____

22. a place to sit _____

23. the nearest in order _____

 **On another sheet of paper, write the list words in order from easiest to hardest to spell.**

# The Missed Kick

 *The* **short-**i **sound** *is found in the word* **miss.**

Read and copy each list word. Circle the letter that makes the short-*i* sound. Then organize the list words by the letter clues.

**List Words**

| | | |
|---|---|---|
| 1. hid | 1. _____ | |
| 2. mix | 2. _____ | **words that begin with *m*** |
| 3. with | 3. _____ | _____ |
| 4. tip | 4. _____ | _____ |
| 5. milk | 5. _____ | _____ |
| 6. miss | 6. _____ | _____ |
| 7. slip | 7. _____ | |
| 8. kick | 8. _____ | |
| 9. kiss | 9. _____ | |
| 10. pick | 10. _____ | |

**words that begin with *m***

_____

_____

_____

_____

**words that have a *p***

_____

_____

_____

_____

**words that begin with *k***

_____

_____

_____

**words that have an *h***

_____

_____

_____

**Challenge Words**

11. into        11. _____

12. trick       12. _____

13. sister      13. _____

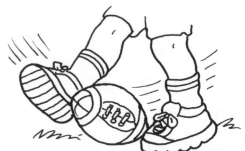

 Circle the word that is spelled correctly.

| | | | | | |
|---|---|---|---|---|---|
| 1. pik | pick | 2. melk | milk | 3. kiss | kis |
| 4. tip | tipp | 5. slep | slip | 6. kik | kick |
| 7. hid | hidd | 8. miks | mix | 9. mis | miss |

 <u>Did he <u>slip</u> and <u>miss</u> the <u>kick</u>?</u>

Scholastic Teaching Resources

Write the list word that matches each clue.

1. I am the past tense of *hide*. I am _____.

2. We rhyme with *sick*. We are _____ and _____.

3. I am part of the dairy food group. I am _____.

4. I begin with the same sound as *wind*. I am _____.

5. I am a synonym for *stir*. I am _____.

6. We rhyme with *flip*. We are _____ and _____.

7. Do this to your mom or dad. I am _____.

8. I am kiss – k + m. I am _____.

Circle each list word hidden in the puzzle. The words go across, down, or diagonally.

| g | m | i | l | k | a | j | l | p | w | e | i | c | e | o |
|---|---|---|---|---|---|---|---|---|---|---|---|---|---|---|
| u | s | o | x | f | x | c | q | b | i | w | f | e | y | z |
| f | l | e | d | m | i | b | t | n | r | c | j | o | d | w |
| p | i | k | i | c | k | p | r | b | m | m | k | i | f | i |
| l | p | i | k | x | a | d | v | c | i | m | i | r | g | t |
| k | u | t | b | d | h | i | d | m | s | r | j | x | n | h |
| v | t | i | p | v | m | g | r | b | s | i | d | i | i | d |
| h | d | i | r | p | n | p | z | k | i | s | s | e | q | i |
| b | c | f | h | a | q | r | t | p | k | a | c | s | h | e |

Write the challenge word that finishes each question.

9. Does Josie's _____ share a bedroom with her?

10. Did you stir the milk _____ the cake mix?

11. Have you learned a new magic _____?

 **On another sheet of paper, write the list words in alphabetical order.**

# Socks With Dots

 *The short-o sound is found in the word sock.*

Read and copy each list word. Circle the letter that makes the short *o* sound. Then organize the list words in rhyming pairs.

 List Words

1. sock
2. mop
3. box
4. spot
5. odd
6. off
7. dot
8. stop
9. fox
10. lock

1. _____   _____   _____
2. _____
3. _____   _____   _____
4. _____
5. _____   _____   _____
6. _____
7. _____
8. _____
9. _____
10. _____   _____   _____

**Which two words do not have a rhyming partner?**

  Challenge Words

11. clock     11. _____
12. cross     12. _____
13. stomp     13. _____

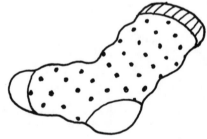

Change the vowel in each word to spell a list word.

1. map _____   2. step _____   3. sack _____

4. fix _____   5. lick _____   6. spit _____

7. add _____

 **My sock with dots is in the box.**

Name _____

 Use a list word to complete each analogy.

1. *Pull* is the antonym for *push. On* is the antonym for _____.

2. A hat goes on your head. A _____ goes on your foot.

3. Scrub a pan. _____ a floor.

4. A knob opens a door. A key opens a _____.

5. *An* is in *can. Ox* is in _____ or _____.

6. *Short* is the antonym for *tall.* _____ is the antonym for *go.*

7. Two, four, and six are even. One, three, and five are _____.

8. A box is square. A _____ is round.

9. A puddle is on the street. A _____ is on the rug.

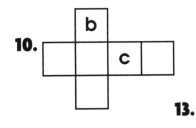 Complete each puzzle with two list words.

10. [crossword: b, c]

11. [crossword: p, f]

12. [crossword: k, x]

13. [crossword: d]

14. [crossword: t, p]

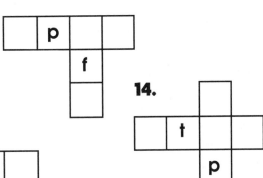

 Write each challenge word three times.

_____   _____   _____

_____   _____   _____

_____   _____   _____

💡 **Find the list words written in some of your favorite books.**

# A Bump in the Road

 The **short-u sound** *is found in the word* **bump**.

Read and copy each list word. Circle the letter that makes the short-*u* sound. Watch for words that use unexpected spellings. Then organize the list by the letters making the short-*u* sound.

**List Words**

1. rub
2. bump
3. come
4. was
5. dump
6. must
7. from
8. dust
9. tub
10. some

| | u | a |
|---|---|---|
| 1. _____ | _____ | |
| 2. _____ | _____ | |
| 3. _____ | _____ | o |
| 4. _____ | _____ | _____ |
| 5. _____ | _____ | |
| 6. _____ | _____ | |
| 7. _____ | | |
| 8. _____ | o_e | |
| 9. _____ | _____ | |
| 10. _____ | _____ | |

**Challenge Words**

11. lunch
12. stuck
13. stung

11. _____
12. _____
13. _____

 Write a list word that begins with the same sound as the picture.

1.  _____
2. _____
3. _____
4. _____
5. _____
6. _____ *and* _____
7. _____
8. _____

 **Riding over the <u>bump</u> <u>must</u> have kicked up <u>some</u> <u>dust</u>.**

Scholastic Teaching Resources

Name _____

 Use two list words to make a rhyme.

**1.** We hit a _____ on our way to the _____.

**2.** Will you give my back a _____ while I sit in the warm _____?

**3.** Achoo! I really _____ begin to _____.

**4.** These cookies are great! When I _____, I will bring _____.

Use the clues to identify the list words. Move the jeeps along the road by shading the answers. The jeep that reaches the end of the road first is the winner!

**5.** more than one

**6.** the past tense of *is*

**7.** a verb that rhymes with *cub*

**8.** starts like *friend*

**9.** jump – j + d

**10.** dirt

**11.** Change the vowel in *most*.

**12.** starts like *candy*

**13.** a noun that rhymes with *cub*

**14.** a ____ in the road

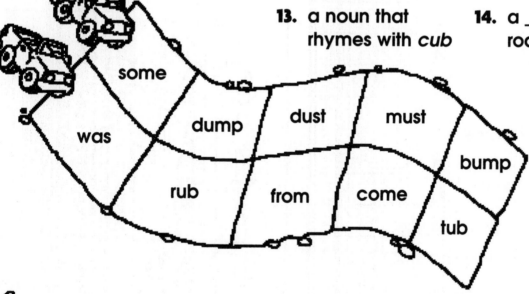

Draw a picture to show each challenge word. Label the picture.

# Who Dropped the Ball?

*Each of these words has a short vowel spelling with one final consonant. Before adding an ending like -ing or -ed, double the final consonant.*

Read and copy each list word. Circle the letter that makes the short vowel sound. Underline the words with double consonants.

 **List Words**

1. tap
2. tapping
3. beg
4. begged
5. skip
6. skipping
7. drop
8. dropped
9. run
10. running

1. _____
2. _____
3. _____
4. _____
5. _____
6. _____
7. _____
8. _____
9. _____
10. _____

**words with no ending**
_____
_____
_____
_____
_____
_____

**words with an -ed ending**
_____
_____
_____

**words with an -ing ending**
_____
_____
_____

**Challenge Words**

11. clapped
12. tripped
13. stopping

11. _____
12. _____
13. _____

Unscramble the letters to spell list words.

1. nunigrn _____
2. dgebge _____
3. propedd _____
4. spik _____
5. snigippk _____
6. patnpig _____

 She <u>dropped</u> the ball when she was <u>running</u> and <u>skipping</u>.

Scholastic Teaching Resources

Name _____

 Write four sentences using at least two list words in each.

1. _____

2. _____

3. _____

4. _____

Crack the code to spell each list word.

| a | b | d | e | g | i | k | n | o | p | r | s | t | u |
|---|---|---|---|---|---|---|---|---|---|---|---|---|---|
| ☆ | ✧ | ✓ | ◉ | ✹ | ✪ | ◷ | ★ | ⇑ | ◯ | ✗ | ⧗ | ▢ | ✺ |

5. _ _ _ _ _ _ _
  ✓ ✗ ⇑ ◯ ◯ ◉ ✓

6. _ _ _ _
  ⧗ ◷ ✪ ◯

7. _ _ _ _ _ _ _ _
  ⧗ ◷ ✪ ◯ ◯ ✪ ★ ✹

8. _ _ _
  ✗ ✺ ★

9. _ _ _ _ _ _ _
  ✗ ✺ ★ ★ ✪ ★ ✹

10. _ _ _ _
  ✓ ✗ ⇑ ◯

11. _ _ _
  ▢ ☆ ◯

12. _ _ _ _ _ _ _
  ▢ ☆ ◯ ◯ ✪ ★ ✹

13. _ _ _ _ _ _
  ✧ ◉ ✹ ✹ ◉ ✓

14. _ _ _
  ✧ ◉ ✹

 Write the challenge word that belongs in each group.

| clap, clapping, | stop, stopped, | trip, tripping, |
|---|---|---|
|  |  |  |

 **On another sheet of paper, make a word search puzzle using the list words. Ask a friend to find the hidden words.**

# A Snake on the Trail

 *The* **long-**a **sound** *can be spelled with the letters* a_e, ai *, or* ay.

Read and copy each list word. Circle the letters that make the long-*a* sound. Watch for a word with an unexpected spelling. Then organize the list words by the letters making the long-*a* sound.

**List Words**

1. say
2. made
3. snake
4. pain
5. away
6. trade
7. train
8. brake
9. trail
10. they

1. _____
2. _____
3. _____
4. _____
5. _____
6. _____
7. _____
8. _____
9. _____
10. _____

**a_e**

_____
_____
_____
_____
_____

unexpected
spelling

_____

**ai**

_____
_____
_____

**ay**

_____

_____

**Challenge Words**

11. raise
12. plate
13. scrape

11. _____
12. _____
13. _____

Write three list words that rhyme with one another.

1. _____       _____       _____

Six other list words have a rhyming partner. Write them below.

2. _____   3. _____   4. _____

_____       _____       _____

 **Did they say the snake on the trail went away?**

Use the list words to complete the letter.

Dear John,

My family went _____ for vacation. We took a _____ to Arizona.

My favorite part was riding horses. We followed a _____ into the desert.

Suddenly my horse had to _____. He saw a _____ on the trail. The

snake was hurt and in _____. I didn't know what to _____. "Stop!"

I called. The others _____ their horses stop. _____ saw the snake,

too. We used a stick to move the snake under a rock. I hope he'll be okay.

Your friend,
Joe

P.S. Do you want to _____ baseball cards?

Follow the clues to complete the puzzle.

**Across**

2. rhymes with *sale*
3. to speak
6. a form of transportation
8. a synonym for *swap*
9. the past tense of *make*

**Down**

1. feel this when you are hurt
2. a list word with an unexpected spelling
4. rhymes with *day*
5. a reptile
7. a synonym for *stop*

Write the challenge word that finishes each analogy.

1. Lower is to move down as _____ is to move up.

2. Cut is to finger as _____ is to knee.

3. Drink is to cup as eat is to _____.

 On another sheet of paper, scramble the letters in each list word. Ask a friend to unscramble the words.

Scholastic Teaching Resources

# A Sleepy Team

 *The* **long**-e **sound** *can be spelled with the letters* e_e, ea, *or* ee.

Read and copy each list word. Circle the letters that make the long-e sound. Then organize the list words by the letters making the long-e sound.

**List Words**

|  |  | e_e | ee |
|---|---|---|---|
| 1. meet | 1. _____ | _____ | _____ |
| 2. each | 2. _____ | _____ | _____ |
| 3. here | 3. _____ | | _____ |
| 4. read | 4. _____ | ea | _____ |
| 5. seen | 5. _____ | _____ | |
| 6. team | 6. _____ | _____ | |
| 7. wheel | 7. _____ | _____ | |
| 8. mean | 8. _____ | _____ | |
| 9. eve | 9. _____ | | |
| 10. sleep | 10. _____ | | |

**Challenge Words**

| | |
|---|---|
| 11. these | 11. _____ |
| 12. easy | 12. _____ |
| 13. please | 13. _____ |

Change one letter in each word to spell a list word. The first one has been done for you.

1. sheep ___sleep___  2. been _____  3. melt _____

4. meal _____  5. tear _____  6. road _____

7. hare _____  8. ewe _____

Change the first and last letters to spell a list word.

9. sheet _____

10. back _____

 <u>Each</u> <u>week</u> the <u>team</u> <u>reads</u> <u>here</u>.

Scholastic Teaching Resources

Circle ten misspelled words. Write them correctly on the lines below.

### A Sleepy Team

Last weak our gymnastics teem met heer. Eech boy and girl had to practice harder than before. We worked as hard as a hamster running on a weel. We did not even have a chance to sleap. At first we thought our coach was meen, but now I have sean what extra work can do for our team. We are all tired, but we are ready for our first gymnastics meet on New Year's Eev. You can rede about it in the newspaper. I hope we do well!

1. _____      2. _____

3. _____      4. _____

5. _____      6. _____

7. _____      8. _____

9. _____      10. _____

Use addition and subtraction to spell each list word.

11. swan – sw + me = _____      12. sell – ll + en = _____

13. help – lp + re = _____      14. she – sh + ve = _____

15. rest – st + ad = _____      16. creep – cr + sl = _____

17. wheat – at + el = _____      18. well – ll + ek = _____

19. itch – it + ea = _____      20. clam – cl + te = _____

Write the challenge word that matches each definition.

21. simple _____

22. used with a request, to show good manners _____

23. used before a plural noun _____

 On another sheet of paper, make a word search puzzle using the list words.

# The Night Sky

 *The* **long-**i **sound** *can be spelled with the letters* i_e, igh, *or* y.

Read and copy each list word. Circle the letters that make the long-*i* sound. Watch for a word that has an unexpected spelling. Then organize the list words by the letters making the long-*i* sound.

| List Words | | i_e | y |
|---|---|---|---|
| 1. sky | 1. _____ | _____ | _____ |
| 2. time | 2. _____ | _____ | _____ |
| 3. right | 3. _____ | _____ | _____ |
| 4. night | 4. _____ | | _____ |
| 5. cry | 5. _____ | **igh** | |
| 6. wide | 6. _____ | _____ | |
| 7. try | 7. _____ | _____ | |
| 8. light | 8. _____ | _____ | |
| 9. slide | 9. _____ | | |
| 10. why | 10. _____ | | |

 **Challenge Words**

| | |
|---|---|
| 11. while | 11. _____ |
| 12. bright | 12. _____ |
| 13. stripe | 13. _____ |

 Circle the word that is spelled correctly.

| | | | | | | | |
|---|---|---|---|---|---|---|---|
| 1. | slyde | slide | 2. | try | trie | 3. | nite | night |
| 4. | right | ryte | 5. | skye | sky | 6. | light | lite |
| 7. | wide | wyde | 8. | cry | crie | 9. | whi | why |

 "That's <u>right</u>. The <u>light</u> in the <u>night</u> <u>sky</u> is the moon."

Write the list word that matches each clue.

1. I am the antonym for *day*. I am _____.

2. Children sit on me at the park. I am a _____.

3. I begin with the same sound as *truck*. I am _____.

4. I am used to ask a question. I am _____.

5. I am a synonym for *weep*. I am _____.

6. I am an antonym for *narrow*. I am _____.

7. We rhyme with *bite*. We are _____ and _____.

8. I am always above you. I am the _____.

9. I tell past, present, and future. I am _____.

Circle each list word hidden in the puzzle. The words go across, down, or diagonally.

| a | q | w | t | s | l | i | d | e | c | r |
|---|---|---|---|---|---|---|---|---|---|---|
| t | t | r | i | d | j | i | s | s | k | w |
| r | p | i | e | d | i | u | g | b | k | h |
| y | l | g | m | y | e | w | o | h | i | y |
| m | f | h | v | e | n | i | g | h | t | s |
| i | n | t | i | l | h | t | g | c | r | y |

Write the challenge word that finishes each sentence.

10. My teacher said, "The American flag has 13 _____s."

11. "Did it rain _____ you were at the beach?" she asked.

12. Michael shouted, "I have a _____ idea!"

  On another sheet of paper, write a story using as many list words as possible.

# Let It Snow!

 *The* **long-**o **sound** *can be spelled with the letters* o_e, oa, *or* ow.

Read and copy each list word. Circle the letters that make the long-*o* sound. Watch for a word that has an unexpected silent letter. Then organize the list words by the letters making the long-*o* sound.

 **List Words**

|  |  | o_e | ow |
|---|---|---|---|
| 1. toad | 1. _____ | _____ | _____ |
| 2. grow | 2. _____ | _____ | _____ |
| 3. nose | 3. _____ | _____ | _____ |
| 4. boat | 4. _____ | | |
| 5. snow | 5. _____ | *oa* | |
| 6. broke | 6. _____ | _____ | |
| 7. close | 7. _____ | _____ | |
| 8. soap | 8. _____ | _____ | |
| 9. coat | 9. _____ | _____ | |
| 10. know | 10. _____ | | |

 **Challenge Words**

| | |
|---|---|
| 11. show | 11. _____ |
| 12. wrote | 12. _____ |
| 13. those | 13. _____ |

👀 Can you find all ten list words hidden two times? Circle them.

brocoatknsoapow       noknowplbrokese       boclosewtoadoatn

snowabrokeknow        bogrowboatlosen       clonosegrowocoat

closeknosnowese       knonoseowsoape        toadyowboatnown

📢 **Did <u>you</u> <u>know</u> she <u>broke</u> her <u>nose</u> in the <u>snow</u>?**

Use a list word to complete each analogy.

1. *Bathing suit* is to *summer* as _____ is to *winter*.

2. A *train* is to *tracks* as a _____ is to *water*.

3. A *knob* is to *door* as a _____ is to *face*.

4. *See* is to *saw* as *break* is to _____.

5. *Rain* is to *warm* as _____ is to *cold*.

6. A *tiger* is to *mammal* as a _____ is to *amphibian*.

7. *Drink* is to *drank* as _____ is to *knew*.

8. *Shampoo* is to *hair* as _____ is to *body*.

Use the clues to identify the list words. Move the sleds down the hill by circling the answers. The sled that reaches the bottom first is the winner!

9. to get bigger

10. used to smell

11. used to clean

12. knit – it + ow

13. antonym for *open*

14. a type of transportation

15. chow – ch + sn

16. used to keep warm

grow

soap

nose

close

boat

know

coat

snow

 Write each challenge word three times.

_____        _____        _____

_____        _____        _____

_____        _____        _____

# Deep in the Hole

 *Some of the common spellings for* **long vowel sounds** *are:*

| a_e | e_e | i_e | o_e |
|-----|-----|-----|-----|
| ai, ay | ea, ee | y, igh | oa, ow |

Read and copy each list word. Circle the letters that make the long vowel sound. Then organize the list words by their long vowel sounds.

 **List Words**

1. deep
2. hole
3. ride
4. meal
5. snail
6. blow
7. game
8. lay
9. goat
10. might

1. _____
2. _____
3. _____
4. _____
5. _____
6. _____
7. _____
8. _____
9. _____
10. _____

**long-*a* sound**
_____
_____
_____

**long-*i* sound**
_____
_____

**long-*e* sound**
_____
_____

**long-*o* sound**
_____
_____
_____

**Challenge Words**

11. globe
12. became
13. smile

11. _____
12. _____
13. _____

Unscramble the letters to spell list words.

1. bowl _____
2. alins _____
3. mega _____
4. alem _____
5. yal _____
6. deir _____
7. tago _____
8. leoh _____
9. githm _____
10. eped _____

 **The snail might lay deep in the hole.**

Write four sentences using at least two list words.

1. _____

2. _____

3. _____

4. _____

Crack the code to spell each list word.

| 1 | 2 | 3 | 4 | 5 | 6 | 7 | 8 | 9 | 10 | 11 | 12 | 13 | 14 | 15 | 16 | 17 |
|---|---|---|---|---|---|---|---|---|----|----|----|----|----|----|----|----|
| g | a | w | r | s | n | i | l | y | d | p | o | t | b | m | h | e |

5. 1–2–15–17

_____

6. 16–12–8–17

_____

7. 8–2–9

_____

8. 15–17–2–8

_____

9. 1–12–2–13

_____

10. 10–17–17–11

_____

11. 15–7–1–16–13

_____

12. 4–7–10–17

_____

13. 14–8–12–3

_____

14. 5–6–2–7–8

_____

 Write the challenge word that belongs in each group.

| become, becoming, | map, atlas, | smirk, frown, |
|---|---|---|
|  |  |  |

 On another sheet of paper, write a definition for each list word.

# The Cute Mule

 *The* **long-**u **sound** *can be spelled with the letters* oo *or* u_e.

Read and copy each list word. Circle the letters that make the long-*u* sound. Watch for a word that has an unexpected spelling. Organize the list words by the letters making the long-*u* sound.

**List Words**

|  | | *oo* | *u_e* |
|---|---|---|---|
| 1. room | 1. _____ | _____ | _____ |
| 2. food | 2. _____ | _____ | _____ |
| 3. tube | 3. _____ | _____ | _____ |
| 4. mule | 4. _____ | _____ | _____ |
| 5. moon | 5. _____ | | _____ |
| 6. rule | 6. _____ | **unexpected spelling** | |
| 7. spoon | 7. _____ | | |
| 8. cute | 8. _____ | _____ | |
| 9. tune | 9. _____ | | |
| 10. who | 10. _____ | | |

**Challenge Words**

11. school   11. _____
12. goose    12. _____
13. scooter  13. _____

Change one letter in each word to spell a list word.

1. cube _____ *or* _____    2. zoom _____

3. tube _____    4. why _____    5. role _____

6. spook _____    7. noon _____    8. fool _____

9. male _____

 <u>Who</u> saw the <u>cute</u> <u>mule</u> eating his <u>food</u>?

Scholastic Teaching Resources

Use a list word to complete each sentence.

1. A _____ is a mammal similar to a donkey.

2. There is a _____ baby mule at the zoo.

3. The baby mule gets anxious when he wants _____.

4. He has plenty of _____ to play in his pen.

5. One zoo _____ is that visitors cannot feed the mule.

6. The _____ revolves around Earth.

7. _____ is going to the football game?

8. My baby sister has learned to eat with a _____.

9. Have you heard this _____ before?

10. I found a _____ of toothpaste in my suitcase.

 Follow the clues to complete the puzzle.

**Across**
  2. rhymes with *groom*
  5. a breakfast utensil
  8. the base word of *ruler*
  10. a synonym for *song*

**Down**
  1. a question word
  3. seen in the night sky
  4. bread, fruit, vegetables
  6. a stubborn mammal
  7. an antonym for *ugly*
  9. rhymes with *cube*

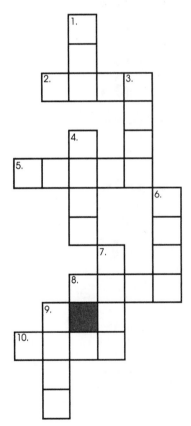

 Write the challenge word that finishes each analogy.

11. A unicycle has one wheel. A _____ has two wheels.

12. A baby cow is a calf. A baby _____ is a gosling.

13. We play on a playground. We learn in a _____.

 **On another sheet of paper, write the list words in order from easiest to hardest to spell.**

Scholastic Teaching Resources

# A True Blue Friend

When the **long-u sound** is found at the end of a word, it can be spelled with the letters *ew or ue*.

Read each list word. Circle the letters that make the long-*u* sound. Watch for a word that has an unexpected spelling. Then organize the list words by the letters making the long-*u* sound.

| List Words | | ew | ue |
|---|---|---|---|
| 1. few | 1. _____ | _____ | _____ |
| 2. new | 2. _____ | _____ | _____ |
| 3. true | 3. _____ | _____ | _____ |
| 4. blue | 4. _____ | _____ | _____ |
| 5. grew | 5. _____ | _____ | |
| 6. flew | 6. _____ | _____ | unexpected spelling |
| 7. glue | 7. _____ | | |
| 8. drew | 8. _____ | | |
| 9. threw | 9. _____ | | _____ |
| 10. two | 10. _____ | | |

Challenge Words

| | |
|---|---|
| 11. due | 11. _____ |
| 12. dew | 12. _____ |
| 13. knew | 13. _____ |

Change the first and last letters of each word to spell a list word.

1. grub _____  2. owl _____  3. let _____ *and* _____

4. sled _____  5. club _____ *and* _____

The <u>bluebird</u> <u>flew</u> over a <u>few</u> <u>new</u> flowers.

Scholastic Teaching Resources

Name

 Circle ten misspelled words. Write them correctly on the lines.

### A True Blue Friend

"Today was a great day at school," Mark said as he thrue the door open. He sat down at the table and took a fue grapes from the bowl. "We drooe pictures to show the parts of a plant. Before I could glew my pictures in place, Drew walked by and brushed them onto the floor. I was so mad! I had to draw tow noow pictures! Then something pretty cool happened. Matthew came over and helped me. We flewe through the work together. I grue less angry then."

Mark's mom replied, "Matthew really is a troo blewe friend."

1. _____   2. _____   3. _____   4. _____   5. _____

6. _____   7. _____   8. _____   9. _____   10. _____

 Use addition and subtraction to spell each list word.

11. flag – ag + ew = _____   12. glad – ad + ue = _____

13. net – t + w = _____   14. toe – oe + wo = _____

15. drum – um + ew = _____   16. grip – ip + ew = _____

17. trap – ap + ue = _____   18. fur – ur + ew = _____

19. crew – c + th = _____   20. blob – ob + ue = _____

 Write the challenge word that matches the definition.

21. drops of water sometimes found on grass early in the morning _____

22. something owed or expected to arrive _____

23. the past tense of *know* _____

 On another sheet of paper, write the list words in alphabetical order.

Scholastic Teaching Resources

# A Good Book

 *The letters* u, oo, *and* ou *can all sound like* oo *in* **good.**

Read and copy each list word. Circle the letters that make the short *oo* sound. Watch for three words that have unexpected spellings. Then organize the list words by the letters that make the short *oo* sound.

**List Words**

1. good
2. book
3. put
4. could
5. look
6. pull
7. would
8. push
9. foot
10. should

**u**

1. _____   _____
2. _____   _____
3. _____   _____
4. _____
5. _____

**oo**

6. _____   _____
7. _____   _____
8. _____   _____
9. _____   _____
10. _____

**Challenge Words**

11. stood      11. _____
12. shook      12. _____
13. cookbook   13. _____

Circle the word that is spelled correctly.

| 1. | shood | should | 2. | louk | look | 3. | put | poot |
| 4. | foot | fout | 5. | cood | could | 6. | gude | good |
| 7. | pul | pull | 8. | book | booke | 9. | woud | would |

 "I **should** **look** for a **good** **book**," Eric said.

10. puch      push

Scholastic Teaching Resources

Name _____

 Write the list word that matches each clue.

1. I am the antonym for *push*. I am _____.

2. When I am plural, I become *feet*. I am _____.

3. I have a homonym that is spelled *wood*. I am _____.

4. Use your eyes to do this. I am _____.

5. I am a synonym for *shove*. I am _____.

6. I am a noun. I am made of paper. I am a _____.

7. I am a three-letter word. I am _____.

8. I am less than *great*. I am _____.

9. We rhyme with *good*. We are _____, _____, and _____.

Circle each list word hidden in the puzzle. The words go across, down, or diagonally.

| g | p | u | s | h | k | w | p | u | t | f |
|---|---|---|---|---|---|---|---|---|---|---|
| b | p | u | o | h | s | b | l | c | j | o |
| o | h | c | l | n | o | i | r | o | t | o |
| o | l | q | v | l | d | u | b | u | o | t |
| k | w | o | u | l | d | c | l | a | k |   |
| f | m | e | d | s | g | o | o | d | t | l |

Write the challenge word that finishes each exclamation.

10. We _____ on the back of a dolphin!

11. The earthquake _____ the house!

12. This is a great _____!

 **Find each of the list words in a few of your favorite books.**

# Which White Shell?

In some words, two letters work together to make one sound.

Read and copy each list word. Circle the letters that make a new sound. Then organize the list words by the letters that make the new sound.

**List Words**

1. wish
2. chase
3. shell
4. shut
5. than
6. chat
7. white
8. them
9. which
10. what

**Challenge Words**

11. there
12. where
13. these

1. _____
2. _____
3. _____
4. _____
5. _____
6. _____
7. _____
8. _____
9. _____
10. _____

11. _____
12. _____
13. _____

*sh*

_____
_____
_____

*ch*

_____
_____
_____

*th*

_____
_____

*wh*

_____
_____
_____

*wh* and *ch*

_____

Can you find all ten list words hidden two times? Circle them.

awshellchwisht       thchasethemack       whshutshchatn

whichthannth         shwhiteafwhatin      chasetwhatente

shutthanewish        prshellenchathir     whichwhitethem

 Which white shell will you give them?

Scholastic Teaching Resources

Name _____

Name _____

**Digraphs** *sh, ch, th,* and *wh*

 Use a list word to complete each analogy.

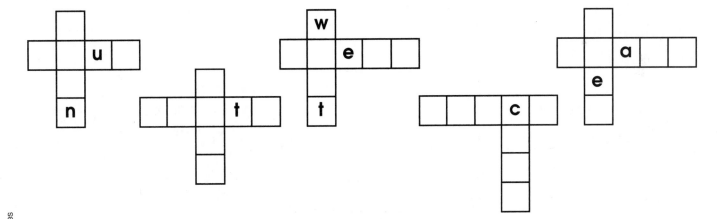

1. To trot is to run. To _____ is to talk.

2. Grass is green. Snow is _____.

3. *Him* means one person. _____ means many people.

4. A rock is found in the dirt. A _____ is found in the ocean.

5. *High* is the antonym for *low*. _____ is the antonym for *open*.

6. *See* is a homonym for *sea*. _____ is a homonym for *witch*.

7. *Chair* rhymes with *hair*. *Pan* rhymes with _____.

8. To run fast is to scurry. To run after is to _____.

9. Make a play in a game. Make a _____ on a star.

10. *Hat* rhymes with *that*. *Hut* rhymes with _____ and _____.

Complete each puzzle with two list words.

Write each challenge word three times.

_____    _____        _____

_____    _____        _____

_____    _____        _____

 **Find each list word in a dictionary. On another sheet of paper, write the list word and the page number where it was found.**

Scholastic Teaching Resources

**Scholastic Success With Spelling   33**

# A Clue to the Treasure Chest

 *In some words two letters work together to make one sound. The* **long-**u **sound** *can be spelled with the letters* oo, u_e, ew, *and* ue. *The* **short** oo **sound** *can be spelled with the letters* u, oo, *and* ou.

Read and copy each list word. Watch for a word that has an unexpected spelling. Then organize the list words by the listed sounds.

**List Words**

| | | long-u sound as in *room* | ch, th, wh, or sh |
|---|---|---|---|
| 1. bush | 1. _____ | | |
| 2. tool | 2. _____ | _____ | _____ |
| 3. thin | 3. _____ | _____ | _____ |
| 4. blew | 4. _____ | _____ | _____ |
| 5. chest | 5. _____ | | _____ |
| 6. took | 6. _____ | short oo sound as in *good* | _____ |
| 7. brush | 7. _____ | | _____ |
| 8. shape | 8. _____ | _____ | |
| 9. clue | 9. _____ | _____ | |
| 10. whale | 10. _____ | | |

**Challenge Words**

| | |
|---|---|
| 11. balloon | 11. _____ |
| 12. choose | 12. _____ |
| 13. shoe | 13. _____ |

Unscramble the letters to spell list words.

1. alhew _____   2. sbuhr _____   3. shetc _____

4. olot _____   5. phesa _____   6. eluc _____

7. elwb _____   8. niht _____   9. shub _____

10. okot _____

 **The** <u>clue</u> **says, "Use the** <u>tool</u> **to open the** <u>chest</u>**."**

Scholastic Teaching Resources

Write four sentences using at least two list words in each.

1. _____

2. _____

3. _____

4. _____

 Riddle time! Use the clues to write each list word in the boxes. When you have finished, the shaded boxes will spell the answer to the riddle.

**What has ten letters and starts with gas?**

1. A square is a _____.

2. rhymes with *blue*

3. a part of the body

4. past tense of *take*

5. a hammer

6. a plant

7. antonym for *thick*

8. an ocean animal

9. homonym for *blue*

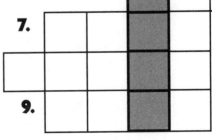

1.

2.

3.

4.

m

5.

6.

7.

8.

9.

 Write the challenge word that belongs in each group.

| sock, boot, | decide, pick, | circus, clown, |
|---|---|---|
| | | |

 On another sheet of paper, make a word search puzzle using the list words. Ask a friend to find all ten words.

# The Hurt Bird

 *The sound a vowel makes often changes when it is followed by an* r.

Read and copy each list word. Circle the "vowel plus r" spellings. Watch for words that have unexpected spellings. Then organize the list words by the number of letters they have.

 **List Words**

1. smart
2. her
3. bird
4. more
5. curl
6. sharp
7. were
8. first
9. hurt
10. your

**three letters**

1. _____    _____
2. _____    _____

**five letters**

_____
_____

**four letters**

3. _____    _____
4. _____    _____
5. _____    _____
6. _____    _____
7. _____    _____
8. _____    _____
9. _____    _____
10. _____

🏆 **Challenge Words**

11. morning      11. _____
12. third        12. _____
13. before       13. _____

 Write a list word that begins with the same sound as the picture.

1.  _____   2. 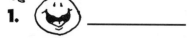 _____   *and* _____

3.  _____   4.  _____   5.  _____

6.  _____   7.  _____   8. 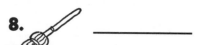 _____

 **Was <u>your</u> <u>bird</u> <u>hurt</u> by the <u>sharp</u> stick?**

Scholastic Teaching Resources

Circle ten misspelled words. Write them correctly on the lines.

Kia was given a berd for her eighth birthday. She named her Sweetie. It was the forst pet Kia had ever had. Sometimes Kia's bird would sit on hir shoulder. "Yor bird is really smurt," everyone told Kia. One day Kia and Sweetie wer sitting on the front porch. A wild bird with a cirl on its head landed nearby. Sweetie flew from Kia's shoulder and onto a branch near the wild bird. The wild bird flew away. Kia waited for Sweetie to fly back, but her bird didn't. Sweetie seemed to be hert. Kia lifted Sweetie down and noticed how sharpe the branch was. Kia said, "You can't fly with the wild birds. They have mor experience than you do, Sweetie." The bird seemed to understand and climbed back onto Kia's shoulder.

1. _____  2. _____  3. _____  4. _____

5. _____  6. _____  7. _____  8. _____

9. _____  10. _____

Follow the clues to play tic-tac-toe. As you find each answer, mark an *X* or *O*. Do you get three in a row?

11. I am the antonym for *dull*. Mark an *O*.
12. I begin like the word *birthday*. Mark an *X*.
13. I come before *second*. Mark an *O*.
14. I am the antonym for *less*. Mark an *X*.
15. I show that a girl owns something. Mark an *O*.
16. I am a synonym for *intelligent*. Mark an *X*.
17. I rhyme with *shirt*. Mark an *O*.
18. I rhyme with *her*. Mark an *X*.
19. I describe a pig's tail. Mark an *O*.

| her | were | hurt |
|---|---|---|
| bird | curl | smart |
| first | more | sharp |

 Draw a picture to illustrate each challenge word. Label the picture.

| | | |
|---|---|---|
| | | |

# The Clown's House

In some words, vowel combinations come together to make a completely new sound. The letters *ou* and *ow* often make the same sound. For example: **out** and **cow**

Read and copy each list word. Circle the *ou* or *ow* spelling. Then organize the list words by either *ou* or *ow*.

### List Words

|  |  | *ou* | *ow* |
|---|---|---|---|
| 1. how | 1. _____ | _____ | _____ |
| 2. clown | 2. _____ | _____ | _____ |
| 3. house | 3. _____ | _____ | _____ |
| 4. down | 4. _____ | _____ | _____ |
| 5. now | 5. _____ | _____ | _____ |
| 6. shout | 6. _____ | | |
| 7. about | 7. _____ | | |
| 8. town | 8. _____ | | |
| 9. count | 9. _____ | | |
| 10. our | 10. _____ | | |

### Challenge Words

| | |
|---|---|
| 11. found | 11. _____ |
| 12. crown | 12. _____ |
| 13. mouth | 13. _____ |

Change the last two letters in each word to spell a list word.

1. shore _____     2. abode _____     3. his _____

4. couch _____     5. torn _____      6. hound _____

7. net _____       8. cloud _____     9. oat _____

 The <u>clown's</u> house is <u>downtown</u> near <u>our</u> <u>house</u>.     10. door _____

Complete the story using each of the list words.

The circus has come to _____! My favorite part is watching the

_____ shoot out of the cannon. We all _____ from 10 _____ to

zero and then yell, "Blast off!" Then we cover _____ ears because the

cannon is loud. You can hear the clown _____, "Wheee," as he flies

over our heads. He flies for _____ two minutes. Then he disappears.

"Where is he _____?" everyone asks. Suddenly, the clown jumps out of

a dog's _____. "Wow! _____ did he do that?" we all wonder.

Use the clues to identify the list words. Move the clowns along the path by shading the answers. The clown that reaches the circus tent first is the winner.

1. the antonym for *up*
2. Where is ____ dog?
3. a circus performer
4. at this time
5. a synonym for *home*
6. smaller than a city
7. 1, 2, 3 . . .
8. a question word
9. not exact
10. a synonym for *yell*

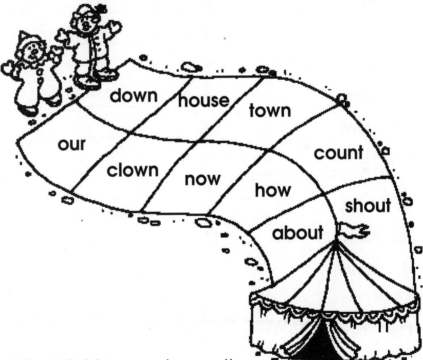

 Write the challenge word that finishes each question.

11. Has he _____ his notebook yet?

12. Can you talk with your _____ closed?

13. Did you notice all of the jewels in the ancient _____?

 **Cut letters from an old newspaper and glue them to another sheet of paper to spell each of the list words.**

# Enjoy the Toy!

 *The letters* oi *and* oy *often make the same sound. For example:* oil *and* boy

Read and copy each list word. Circle the *oi* or *oy* spelling. Then organize the list words by either *oi* or *oy*.

 **List Words**                                            *oi*                    *oy*

**1.** oil      1. _____    _____    _____

**2.** boy      2. _____    _____    _____

**3.** toy      3. _____    _____    _____

**4.** join     4. _____    _____    _____

**5.** soil     5. _____    _____

**6.** joy      6. _____    _____

**7.** boil     7. _____

**8.** enjoy    8. _____

**9.** coin     9. _____

**10.** point   10. _____

🏆 **Challenge Words**

**11.** noise   11. _____

**12.** voice   12. _____

**13.** annoy   13. _____

👓 Circle the word that is spelled correctly.

| 1. | joi | joy | 2. | soyl | soil | 3. | toy | toye |
|---|---|---|---|---|---|---|---|---|
| 4. | koin | coin | 5. | boy | boiy | 6. | joyn | join |
| 7. | enjoy | injoy | 8. | oil | oyl | 9. | boyl | boil |
|  |  |  |  |  |  | 10. | poynt | point |

 The <u>boy</u> will <u>enjoy</u> the <u>toy</u> <u>coin</u>.

Scholastic Teaching Resources

Name _____

 **Diphthongs** *oi* **and** *oy*

 Use a list word to complete each analogy.

1. A fish lives in water. A flower lives in _____.
2. *Woman* is to *man* as *girl* is to _____.
3. *Cat* is to *at* as *boil* is to _____.
4. The nose is part of an airplane. The _____ is part of a pencil.
5. Water will freeze when it is cold. Water will _____ when it is hot.
6. *Rough* is the antonym of *smooth*. *Dislike* is the antonym of _____.
7. To separate is to break apart. To _____ is to come together.
8. Sadness is pain. Happiness is _____.
9. A tire is made of rubber. A _____ is made of metal.
10. A dog plays with a bone. A child plays with a _____.

 Use the Braille code to spell each list word.

| b | c | e | i | j | l | n | o | p | s | t | y |
|---|---|---|---|---|---|---|---|---|---|---|---|

11. __ __ __
12. __ __ __ __
13. __ __ __ __
14. __ __ __
15. __ __ __
16. __ __ __ __
17. __ __ __ __ __
18. __ __ __
19. __ __ __ __
20. __ __ __ __ __

 Write the challenge word that finishes each analogy.

21. *Scream* is a synonym for *yell*. *Bug* is a synonym for _____.
22. You walk with your feet. You sing with your _____.
23. You hear whispers in the library. You hear _____ on the playground.

 **Write a story using as many list words as possible.**

Scholastic Teaching Resources

41Scholastic Success With Spelling   41

Name _____

# There Goes the Ball!

 *The letters* aw *make the sound in the word* **law**. *The letters* all *make the sound in the word* **ball**. *These are two different sounds.*

Read and copy each list word. Circle the *aw* or *all* spellings. Then organize the list words by either *aw* or *all*.

**List Words**                                              *aw*                    *all*

1. tall        1. _____      _____      _____
2. jaw         2. _____      _____      _____
3. ball        3. _____      _____      _____
4. hall         4. _____      _____      _____
5. paw        5. _____      _____      _____
6. saw        6. _____
7. call         7. _____
8. draw       8. _____
9. yawn       9. _____
10. fall        10. _____

**Challenge Words**

11. dawn      11. _____
12. claw      12. _____
13. hawk      13. _____

 Write a list word that begins with the same letter as the picture.

1.  _____    2.  _____    3.  _____
4. 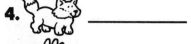 _____   5. 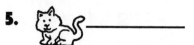 _____    6. 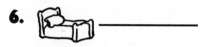 _____
7.  _____   8. 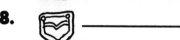 _____   9.  _____

 **I <u>saw</u> the <u>ball</u> <u>fall</u> down the <u>hall</u>.**

Scholastic Teaching Resources

Name _____

 Write the list word that matches each clue.

1. I am an animal's foot. I am a _____.

2. You do this when you are sleepy. I am a _____.

3. I am part of your face. I am a _____.

4. I am a season called autumn. I am _____.

5. I am an antonym for *short*. I am _____.

6. I am the past tense for *see*. I am _____.

7. I am shaped like a sphere. I am a _____.

8. I am the present tense of *drew*. I am _____.

9. I may be part of your school or house. I am a _____.

10. Your mother may do this at dinnertime. She may _____ you.

 Circle each list word hidden in the puzzle. The words go across, down, or diagonally.

| r | h | j | p | d | c | f | a | l | l | d |
|---|---|---|---|---|---|---|---|---|---|---|
| b | t | a | y | p | a | w | b | j | a | r |
| c | y | b | l | f | l | t | l | a | c | a |
| d | a | h | c | l | l | y | a | w | l | w |
| k | w | s | a | w | s | f | s | l | p | l |
| f | n | e | a | l | l | r | j | p | l | l |

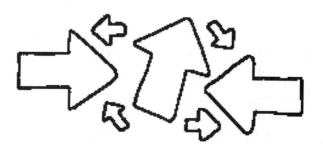

Change the last two letters in each word to spell a challenge word.

11. clip _____

12. hand _____

13. damp _____

 **On another sheet of paper, write the list words in rhyming groups. Brainstorm more rhyming words for each list and write them.**

Scholastic Teaching Resources

# The Girl's Small Horse

*Many letters may work together to make a new sound.*
*Remember these:* ar  er  ir  or  ur  ou  ow  aw  all  oi  oy

Read and copy each list word. Circle the letters that work together. Then organize the list words by their vowel sounds.

 **List Words**

| | | | **words with vowel + r** | **words with all or aw** |
|---|---|---|---|---|
| **1.** art | **1.** _____ | | _____ | _____ |
| **2.** straw | **2.** _____ | | _____ | _____ |
| **3.** girl | **3.** _____ | | _____ | _____ |
| **4.** south | **4.** _____ | | _____ | |
| **5.** small | **5.** _____ | | _____ | **word with oi** |
| **6.** horse | **6.** _____ | | _____ | _____ |
| **7.** frown | **7.** _____ | | | |
| **8.** sister | **8.** _____ | | **words with ou or ow** | |
| **9.** turn | **9.** _____ | | _____ | |
| **10.** foil | **10.** _____ | | _____ | |

🏆 **Challenge Words**

**11.** purple      **11.** _____

**12.** round      **12.** _____

**13.** shirt      **13.** _____

👀 Unscramble the letters to spell list words.

**1.** rat _____      **2.** ilof _____      **3.** stohu _____

**4.** nutr _____      **5.** mlsla _____      **6.** ritses _____

**7.** norwf _____      **8.** resoh _____      **9.** wasrt _____

 The <u>small</u> <u>girl</u> may <u>frown</u> when she sees the <u>horse</u> <u>turn</u>.      **10.** ligr _____

Write four sentences using at least two list words in each.

1. _____

2. _____

3. _____

4. _____

Riddle time! Use the clues to write each list word in the boxes. When you have finished, the shaded boxes will spell the answer to the riddle.

**What do you call a crazy spaceman?**

1. helps you take a drink

2. change directions

3. antonym for *big*

4. an animal

5. a class at school

6. antonym for *boy*

7. wrap food in this

8. rhymes with *clown*

9. a direction

10. a girl in your family

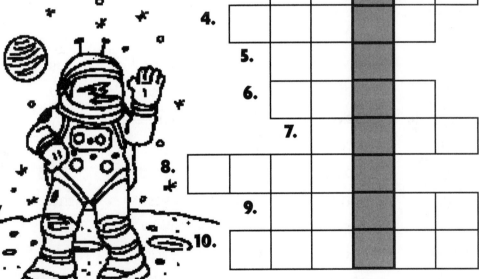

Write the challenge word that belongs in each group.

| yellow, blue, | square, rectangular, | shoes, pants, |
|---|---|---|
| | | |

 **On another sheet of paper, write the definition for each of the list words.**

Name _____

# Master Spelling List

| | | | | | | |
|---|---|---|---|---|---|---|
| about | clap | foot | light | pick | slide | tool |
| after | close | fox | lock | point | slip | town |
| art | clown | from | look | pull | small | toy |
| ask | clue | frown | made | push | smart | trade |
| away | coat | game | map | put | snail | trail |
| ball | coin | girl | mask | read | snake | train |
| bed | come | glue | meal | ride | snow | true |
| beg | could | goat | mean | right | soap | try |
| begged | count | good | meet | room | sock | tub |
| bend | cry | grew | met | rub | soil | tube |
| best | curl | grow | might | rule | some | tune |
| bird | cute | hall | milk | run | south | turn |
| black | deep | has | miss | running | spoon | two |
| blew | dot | have | mix | sack | spot | was |
| blow | down | her | moon | said | stop | went |
| blue | draw | here | mop | saw | straw | were |
| boat | drew | hid | more | say | tall | whale |
| boil | drop | hole | mule | seen | tap | what |
| book | dropped | horse | must | send | tapping | wheel |
| box | dump | house | nest | shape | team | which |
| boy | dust | how | new | sharp | tent | white |
| brake | each | hurt | night | shell | than | who |
| broke | enjoy | jaw | nose | should | them | why |
| brush | eve | join | now | shout | they | wide |
| bump | fall | joy | odd | shut | thin | wish |
| bush | few | kick | off | sister | threw | with |
| call | first | kiss | oil | skip | time | would |
| chase | flew | know | our | skipping | tip | yawn |
| chat | foil | last | pain | sky | toad | yet |
| chest | food | lay | paw | sleep | took | your |

Scholastic Teaching Resources

## Page 4

three letters: map, ask, has; four letters: last, sack, clap, mask, have; five letters: after, black; 2. mask; 3. clap; 4. black; 5. last; 6. map; 7. has; 8. sack; 9. have

## Page 5

has; black; Last; have; ask; mask; map; clap; After; sack; 1. ask; 2. black; 3. last; 4. after; 5. has; 6. sack; 7. clap; 8. have; 9. mask; 10. stamp; 11. stand; 12. backpack

## Page 6

t: tent, met, went, nest, yet, best; d: send, bed, bend, said; 1. tent, went; 2. met, yet; 3. send, bend; 4. bed, said; 5. nest, best

## Page 7

1. tent; 2. bend; 3. best; 4. bed; 5. said; 6. nest; 7. send; 8. met; 9. went; 10. yet; 12. tent; 13. met; 14. bed; 15. send; 16. said; 17. bend; 18. yet; 19. nest; 20. went; 21. else; 22. bench; 23. next

## Page 8

m: mix, milk, miss; p: tip, slip, pick; k: kick; kiss; h: hid, with; 1. pick; 2. milk; 3. kiss; 4. tip; 5. slip; 6. kick; 7. hid; 8. mix; 9. miss

## Page 9

1. hid; 2. kick, pick; 3. milk; 4. with; 5. mix; 6. tip, slip; 7. kiss; 8. miss; 9. sister; 10. into; 11. trick

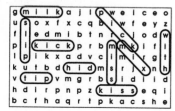

## Page 10

sock, lock; mop, stop; box, fox; spot, dot; odd, off; 1. mop; 2. stop; 3. sock; 4. fox; 5. lock; 6. spot; 7. odd

## Page 11

1. off; 2. sock; 3. mop; 4. lock; 5. box, fox; 6. stop; 7. odd; 8. dot; 9. spot; 10. sock, box; 11. spot, off; 12. lock, fox; 13. odd, dot; 14. stop, mop

## Page 12

u: rub, bump, tub, dust, dump, must; o_e: come, some; a: was; o: from; 1. some; 2. must; 3. rub or bump; 4. bump; 5. was; 6. from; 7. come; 8. dump, dust

## Page 13

1. bump, dump; 2. rub, tub; 3. must, dust; 4. come, some; 5. some; 6. was; 7. rub; 8. from; 9. dump; 10. dust; 11. must; 12. come; 13. tub; 14. bump

## Page 14

no ending: tap, beg, skip, drop, run; -ed: begged, dropped; -ing: tapping, skipping, running; 1. running; 2. begged; 3. dropped; 4. skip; 5. skipping; 6. tapping

## Page 15

5. dropped; 6. skip; 7. skipping; 8. run; 9. running, 10. drop; 11. tap; 12. tapping; 13. begged; 14. beg; clapped, stopping, tripped

## Page 16

a_e: made, snake, trade, brake; ai: pain, train, trail; ay: say, away; unexpected spelling: they; 1. say, away, they; 2. made, trade; 3. snake, brake; 4. pain, train

## Page 17

away, train, trail, brake, snake, pain, say, made, They, trade; 1. raise; 2. scrape; 3. plate

## Page 18

e_e: here, eve; ea: each, read, team, mean; ee: meet, seen, wheel, sleep; 1. sleep; 2. seen; 3. meet; 4. mean; 5. team; 6. read; 7. here; 8. eve; 9. wheel; 10. each

## Page 19

1. week; 2. team; 3. here; 4. Each; 5. wheel; 6. sleep; 7. mean; 8. seen; 9. Eve; 10. read; 11. mean; 12. seen; 13. here; 14. eve; 15. read; 16. sleep; 17. wheel; 18. week; 19. each; 20. team; 21. easy; 22. please; 23. these

## Page 20

i_e: time, wide, slide; igh: right, night, light; y: sky, cry, try, why; 1. slide; 2. try; 3. night; 4. right; 5. sky; 6. light; 7. wide; 8. cry; 9. why

## Page 21

1. night; 2. slide; 3. try; 4. why; 5. cry; 6. wide; 7. right, light; 8. sky; 9. time; 10. stripe; 11. while; 12. bright

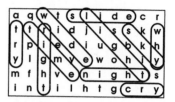

## Page 22

o_e: nose, broke, close; oa: toad, boat, soap, coat; ow: grow, snow, know; coat, soap; know, broke; close, toad; snow, broke, know; grow, boat; nose, grow, coat; close, snow; nose, soap; toad, boat

## Page 23

1. coat; 2. boat; 3. nose; 4. broke; 5. snow; 6. toad; 7. know; 8. soap; 9. grow; 10. nose; 11. soap; 12. know; 13. close; 14. boat; 15. snow; 16. coat

## Page 24

long a: snail, game, lay; long e: deep, meal; long i: ride, might; long o: hole, blow, goat; 1. blow; 2. snail; 3. game; 4. meal; 5. lay; 6. ride; 7. goat; 8. hole; 9. might; 10. deep

## Page 25

5. game; 6. hole; 7. lay; 8. meal; 9. goat; 10. deep; 11. might; 12. ride; 13. blow; 14. snail; became, globe, smile

## Page 26

oo: room, food, moon, spoon; u_e: tube, mule, rule, cute, tune; unexpected spelling: who; 1. cute, tube; 2. room; 3. tune; 4. who; 5. rule; 6. spoon; 7. moon; 8. food; 9. mule

**Page 27**
1. mule; 2. cute; 3. food;
4. room; 5. rule; 6. moon;
7. Who; 8. spoon; 9. tune;
10. tube; 11. scooter;
12. goose; 13. school

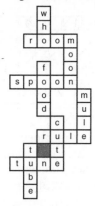

**Page 28**
ew: few, new, grew, flew, drew, threw; eu: true, blue, glue; unexpected spelling: two; 1. true; 2. two; 3. new and few; 4. flew; 5. blue and glue

**Page 29**
1. threw; 2. few; 3. drew;
4. glue; 5. two; 6. new;
7. flew; 8. grew; 9. true;
10. blue; 11. flew; 12. glue;
13. new; 14. two; 15. drew;
16. grew; 17. true; 18. few;
19. threw; 20. blue;
21. dew; 22. due; 23. knew

**Page 30**
u: put, pull, push; oo: good, book, look, foot; ou: could, would, should;
1. should; 2. look; 3. put;
4. foot; 5. could; 6. good;
7. pull; 8. book; 9. would;
10. push

**Page 31**
1. pull; 2. foot; 3. would;
4. look; 5. push; 6. book;
7. put; 8. good; 9. could, should, would; 10. stood;
11. shook; 12. cookbook

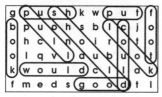

**Page 32**
sh: wish, shell, shut; ch: chase, chat; th: than, them; wh: white, what; wh and ch: which; shell, wish; chase, them; shut, chat; which, than; white, what; chase, what; shut, than; wish; shell, chat; which, white, them

**Page 33**
1. chat; 2. white; 3. Them;
4. shell; 5. Shut; 6. Which;
7. than; 8. chase; 9. wish;
10. shut, what

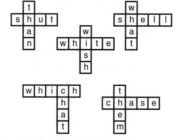

**Page 34**
room: tool, blew, clue; good: bush, took; ch, th, wh, or sh: bush, thin, chest, brush, shape, whale; 1. whale; 2. brush; 3. chest; 4. tool; 5. shape; 6. clue; 7. blew; 8. thin; 9. bush; 10. took

**Page 35**
1. shape; 2. clue; 3. chest;
4. took; 5. tool; 6. bush;
7. thin; 8. whale; 9. blew; automobile; shoe, choose, balloon

**Page 36**
three: her; four: bird, more, curl, were, hurt, your; five: smart, sharp, first;
1. smart; 2. her, hurt;
3. first; 4. were; 5. bird;
6. curl; 7. sharp; 8. more

**Page 37**
1. bird; 2. first; 3. her;
4. Your; 5. smart; 6. were;
7. curl; 8. hurt; 9. sharp;
10. more; 11. sharp;
12. bird; 13. first; 14. more;
15. her; 16. smart;
17. hurt; 18. were; 19. curl

**Page 38**
ou: house, shout, about, count, our; ow: how, clown, down, now, town;
1. shout; 2. about; 3. how;
4. count; 5. town; 6. house;
7. now; 8. clown;
9. our; 10. down

**Page 39**
town, clown, count, down, our, shout, about, now, house, How; 1. down;
2. our; 3. clown; 4. now;
5. house; 6. town;
7. count; 8. how; 9. about;
10. shout; 11. found;
12. mouth; 13. crown

**Page 40**
oi: oil, join, soil, boil, coin, point; oy: boy, toy, joy, enjoy; 1. joy; 2. soil; 3. toy;
4. coin; 5. boy; 6. join;
7. enjoy; 8. oil; 9. boil;
10. point

**Page 41**
1. soil; 2. boy; 3. oil;
4. point; 5. boil; 6. enjoy;
7. join; 8. joy; 9. coin;
10. toy; 11. oil; 12. coin;
13. boil; 14. toy; 15. boy;
16. soil; 17. enjoy; 18. joy;
19. join; 20. point;
21. annoy; 22. voice;
23. noise

**Page 42**
aw: jaw, paw, saw, draw, yawn; tall: all, ball, hall, call, fall; 1. saw; 2. jaw;
3. draw; 4. fall; 5. call;
6. ball; 7. hall; 8. paw;
9. yawn

**Page 43**
1. paw; 2. yawn; 3. jaw;
4. fall; 5. tall; 6. saw;
7. ball; 8. draw; 9. hall;
10. call; 11. claw;
12. hawk; 13. dawn

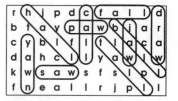

**Page 44**
vowel + r: art, girl, horse, sister, turn; ou or ow: south, frown; all or aw: straw, small; oi: foil; 1. art;
2. foil; 3. south; 4. turn;
5. small; 6. sister; 7. frown;
8. horse; 9. straw; 10. girl

**Page 45**
1. straw; 2. turn; 3. small;
4. horse; 5. art; 6. girl;
7. foil; 8. frown; 9. south;
10. sister; an astronut; purple, round, shirt

Scholastic Teaching Resources